Copyright © 2
All rights
No portion of this book r
form without permission from the publisher, except
as permitted by U.S. copyright law.
For permissions contact:

PO Box 613401
Miami, FL 33261

The Morning I Dumped Sugar & Met A Healthier ME

J. Jerome

Acknowledgment

To God be the glory.

Forever grateful to the memories of my amazing great-gran Ismanie, and grandma "mama" Grace's unconditional love. Their genuine encouragement and wise counsel continue to guide all my steps. Though I miss them more than meager words could ever expressed, I feel better knowing that my loving guardian angels are closely watching over me.

This book is lovingly dedicated to the other strong, beautiful and courageous women, who have always been the backbone of my little life. That includes but not limited to my wonderful mom, who is my role model of a determined and passionate entrepreneurial woman; my sweet and funny auntie Ma; my confident and caring auntie Nounoune; my fearless and witty auntie Evie; my vivacious little sis, remarkable cousins and awesome girlfriends. I'm truly lucky to say that this list is endless; though more importantly, that who I am today, wouldn't exist without their support.

Since family is more than blood... if we are fortunate, we get the privilege to grow our family, as we experience this earth. These last two weeks, would not have been as manageable, without my dear friend/chosen cousin, Rosie. I'm so thankful for you and your sweet children.

Thank you all!!

Table of Contents

Acknowledgment	3
Table of Contents	5
Preface	6
Prologue	7
Bittersweet Truth	9
System Reset	11
Elimination Process	13
Nutrition Education	15
Individualized Plan	18
Healthier Choices	24
Positive Lifestyle	27
Weight Loss	29
Lessons Learned	31

Preface

I had been contemplating writing this little book for a while now; but somehow, various other projects kept pushing it off to the side. Then this month, I started physical therapy for a recent shoulder surgery, and revisited the idea just as a way to keep my mind off the terrible pain, and many unanticipated challenges. Ironically, here I am, two weeks later, prefacing the finished book, with vitality and renewed hope for full recovery.

As I was awkwardly but happily typing away, I could hear the angelic voice of my beloved mama Grace kindly reminding me that everything happens, when it needs to happen. I don't know about you, but I sure love those beautiful moments, that Oprah calls our "aha moments". You see, I initially wanted to write this book, in the hope that it might encourage someone who's looking for inspiration; only to end up getting motivated myself, during that writing process, at a most difficult and vulnerable time. To me, that's life in a nutshell!

Prologue

I woke up one morning, walked into my kitchen, looked around, and just started throwing all the sugar I had in my house, into the trash can. Then, as if further compelled, I determinedly tied the nearly empty trash bag, and marched it right outside to the garbage bin; somehow impervious to my state of dress and raging rain. It was almost as if I needed to ensure complete removal of all sugar from my field of vision.

Truth is, sweets having been my kryptonite, my entire life, I could absolutely understand that compulsion. Even during my teens, I was never a so called "unhealthy" eater, but presented with some sweets? I could easily lose a good bit of my common sense. To make matter worse, I was diagnosed with Polycystic ovarian syndrome (PCOS) when I was 14; from that point on, I struggled terribly with inflammation, acne, borderline insulin resistance and more… as can often be the case with PCOS. So considering the above mentioned issues, my overall health was actually decent, and my doctors felt that I managed my weight remarkably well. Yes, I indeed always tried my best; however, I just couldn't shake off the feeling that I was not living to my optimal health. Does that make sense?

So over the years, I started paying more attention to the details of my health, and especially my nutrition. Still, that feeling that I wasn't functioning at my best persisted, and I just couldn't seem to clearly identify nor resolve it. Well, that was until the weeks that followed that faithful morning in my kitchen with the sugar and trash bag... ring a bell?

In fact, let's take a step back, and start from the beginning in a format that will provide you a simple, yet more detailed understanding into that little journey to a healthier ME.

Bittersweet Truth

"The first step in solving a problem, is to recognize that it does exist." Zig Ziglar

If we were being completely honest with ourselves, we would all agree that a big part of most inherited eating habits, are a bit unhealthy. Now don't get me wrong, as an island girl, who grew up with some of the best cooks, I can certainly attest to the pure deliciousness that can make such food so addictive. However, as Zig Ziglar stated all those years ago, in order to make the necessary changes that would led to a healthier ME, I had to first recognized that some of my eating habits were an impediment to the healthiest possible lifestyle.

Though I'll be the first to admit that acknowledging this problem isn't as easy as it sounds; since by the time we've reached early adulthood, we are already conditioned to most of our likes and dislikes. As a matter of fact, I think that it is downright difficult for most of us to take that first step, and admit that bittersweet truth.

——

Once we've acknowledged the problem, we can begin to focus on how to effectively achieve the necessary changes. However, I think that in order for all those changes to be lasting, we must always try to identify and understand the personal significance of that transformation. It's similar to an identification process in business that's often referred to as the 5 Ws and 1 H "who, what, where, when, why, and how". In this case, the emphasis is on the "why". For me, it came down to my simply wanting to become the best version of myself, while living the healthiest possible lifestyle. As I have gotten older, I started to realize that for me, being a healthier ME meant the whole me... inside and out. Right on the tail of that realization, came the even bigger truth, that all my choices directly and proportionately defined my lifestyle.

Therefore, I decided to take control over my quality of life, by consciously and constantly making better choices. Now, it goes without saying that nutrition and diet, are among some of the most important decisions that we all encounter, on a daily basis. Hence, establishing healthier eating habits, was at the top of my list, on that new path to better health.

System Reset

"Be like a tree and let the dead leaves drop."
Rumi

I have always been a firm believer in periodically pushing the reset button. Thus came that defining moment of getting rid of all the sugar in my house. As empowering as that felt, it was still only the opening act. So once I was ready to delve into the body of that process, I really felt compelled to "reset" my GI system; maybe it's a residual effect from an upbringing by THE BEST Caribbean grandmother. I can still recall every signature concoction, and her bi-yearly detox routines. Anyhow, I really wanted to create a clean slate for the upcoming steps.

Now, as an adult, I had done various other detox plans, but this time, I wanted something more in depth. So after some pondering, I decided to do a multifaceted cleanse, to include varying degrees of fasting. During the last 72 hours of that cleansing process, I only consumed water and electrolytes. Yes, I know that sounds a bit extreme, but for me it was crucial to the success of the next phase that I had in mind. I must pause here for a quick second to remind you how important it is to meet with your primary care physician before ever embarking on any lifestyle changes, especially dietary.

Throughout history we can clearly observe a variation of detox and/or fasting elements, in the overall lifestyle of most cultures with healthier dietary habits. Unfortunately, some of those cultures have lost a bit of those important customs to the evolution of the western pattern diet. I won't go any further into this aspect of dietary habits here, as we'll cover it in a latter chapter. For now, suffice it to say that most people if not everyone, should undergo some kind of periodic cleansing/detoxification, in support of their overall health.

Even before my multifaceted cleanse ended, I could feel a difference in my wellbeing. There was an almost soothing feeling in my abdomen, and an increase in mental acuity. If done right, this phase should be just like the demolition and clearing out debris aspect, of a renovation project. Its main purpose is to help you establish a clean canvas for the desired improvements.

Elimination Process

"The only definitive test for food allergy is whether a person can consume that food without an adverse reaction." David Fleischer

Now that I have done a full and proper cleanse, my next concern was to identify any food allergy and/or sensitivities, by slowly re-introducing food into my system in a streamlined method. This step can be a really tedious process, however I truly believe it is one of the most essential elements to getting on a healthier plan. As a matter of fact, even for those who are always practicing healthy eating habits, it might be a good idea to complete this process every once a while, as food production changes, and so does the human body. It's well known, that you can digest certain food from birth without problems, then all of a sudden, you can develop a particular allergy or sensitivity to them. So, it is a good habit to periodically reset your system. To me, there are no other ways to fully know how your body truly reacts to any particular food.

——

As it turned out, I discovered a number of allergies and sensitivities to many food groups. For instance, I'm allergic to certain shellfish and nuts. In addition, sensitivity kicks in, if I consume too much processed starch; often in the form of bad heartburn. Also, I simply cannot consume meat on a regular basis, without experiencing mild nausea. Furthermore, my tolerance for dairy changes periodically. These are just a few of my discoveries, and it was very enlightening for me to learn these things about my body. We all theoretically know about top allergens, and other food that some people can't tolerate, but I think it is powerful to know specifically what does or does not actually work for our unique digestive tracts. Yes, we are all human beings, with similar systems, but it's a universal truth that our respective body does indeed react differently to certain things.

Again, it was a long and meticulous process to monitor each food group; but for the elimination study to be effective, it had to be done right. For me, I think it is absolutely worth taking that time to do the elimination process, because you get clear, individualized information for yourself. Having done it several times now, I truly believe that it's essential to my flourishing health.

Nutrition Education

"Good nutrition will prevent 95 percent of all disease." Linus Pauling

Like many, I believe that more than ever, it's crucial to properly educate ourselves on nutrition. As everything evolves, we've gotten further and further away, from real food. In fact, the relational effects of commercialization and food advertising, have continuously been more negative than positive. Now, factor in the real phenomenon of information overload that we all face in today's digital world, and it's a major concern for those who care about their health.

Earlier, we talked about the traditional eating habits of certain cultures and the negative changes that they've gone through due in part to the western pattern diet. For instance, I have seen how that trend has impacted some of the dietary customs in the Caribbean, including my home country of Haiti. These days, you see more buying of frozen meat and processed food, compare to how my grandmother used to buy farm raised meat, vegetables, and prepare them from scratch. Now, I know that there's more to it than what we've mentioned here. Yes, nowadays both parents often work outside of the home, and people no longer live close to their grandparents, aunties, who can help... so they are looking for convenience when it comes to buying and preparing food for their families. I'm only focusing on the other aspect because that's mostly where it all started.

Fortunately, in recent years, especially since Covid, there seems to be a reawakening, and people appear more mindful of what they consume, how it's being grown, packaged and sold. It's so good to see, and I hope it's not just a trend that's going to disappear in a couple of years; but that it's rather a change that's here to stay. If we are truly what we eat, then we must prioritize nutrition education, so we can make the best informed decision, to nurture our health.

——

Now, because information overload, will likely continue to be a major problem, we must all learn to cautiously navigate through the plethora of often false and misleading data that's out there. I'm always careful to select only verified and factual results about any research. By the same token, we still have to remember that even the best science-based hypothesis goes through modifications. Frankly, that is another huge challenge in keeping ourselves informed on nutrition and health news. Something that might be considered good for our health today, can tomorrow be categorized as the worst thing for us to use. Which bring us back to my earlier point on the importance of personally trying things out for yourself, and paying attention to what your body is communicating to you. You must be the leading consultant on what's best for you and your health. Even when it comes to medical care, I operate on the basis, that it's a collaboration between me and my physicians. I try to stay connected to my body, so that I can notice when something isn't working and/or doesn't feel right.

Individualized Plan

"What you find at the end of your fork is more powerful than anything you'll find at the bottom of a pill bottle." Mary Buchan

Since that sugary morning in my little kitchen had unexpectedly turned into a transformative journey, my ultimate goal became to create a balanced, individualized nutrition guide, to help nourish my body and better support my health goals.

Of course, by that point, I had steadily stopped consuming anything that could be harmful to my body and wellbeing. Also, any food that no longer belonged or served a purpose in my sustenance, had been cleaned out and donated to favorite local food pantries. I was already dedicated to a good lifestyle change, but became even more excited as I began to devise my personal nutrition guidelines.

I had no desire to follow any of the trending and short-term diets. Rather, based on all my individual testing and research studies, discussed in the prior chapters... I had several core objectives in mind for my plan.

- I wanted plant-focused, nutrients rich and balanced food for all my meals. I wasn't a huge

fan of meat to begin with, but became even less so after my elimination process. When and if I decided to moderately consume meat, it would have to be all grass-fed and hormone free.
- I pledged to myself to try my best to only purchase fresh, locally and naturally grown produce. Yes, it is often more expensive to buy the kind that I just mentioned, but I believe that my health is worth it, even if I have to remove something else from my budget.
- I didn't want to eat anything with an ingredient list that I could not fully read and understand. I had always done the quick "customary" peek, but the first time I truly read the label on a product that I was buying... I was absolutely shocked. Wow, what an eye opener! Today, I won't buy even a bottle of water without reading it's label; it's that simple for me.
- I hoped to continue to be open to trying new food... which included some unprocessed grains, meat and dairy alternatives. That was probably easier for me than it might have been for most other people, because frankly with great seasonings and cooking techniques, I can easily adapt/adjust, and actually enjoy most food; especially if I know that it's good for me.
- I wanted to try and plan all my meals around whatever was in season. The benefit is that most

things that are in season, are usually cheaper; also often of better quality and ripeness.

- I desired to prepare and cook at least 80% of my meals, and only occasionally go out to restaurants for a special celebration. I never really minded cooking before, but just the thoughts of the benefits of knowing exactly what I was going to put in body, certainly rendered the process even more enticing to me.
- I was going to be mindful of the thin line that sometimes separate healthy eating habits, from unhealthy obsessions and even disorders. I never wanted to be so rigid, that I couldn't enjoy occasional treats, dinner invitations, nor going out to a nice restaurant for special celebrations. Life is about healthy balance and moderation.
- Last, but certainly not the least, I planned to implement intuitive intermittent fasting into my eating habits. I had experienced firsthand the positive effects that fasting had on my body, and wanted to continue that practice in a safe manner. I'd come to realize that at specific times, we often eat just because it's customary, and not necessarily because we are hungry. So, if I'm not hungry, I simply wait until I do, thereby allowing my system more time to digest and rest. At this point, I often only really feel like eating two good quality meals a day. First one, usually between

11:30 & noon; second one, around 6:00 to 7:00. Of course it can also varies based on my schedule for any particular day.

——

Now, I knew for a fact that it was going to be challenging, especially when it was all happening right before the year-end holidays. Nevertheless, empowered by the knowledge and the initial changes, I was very determined to do whatever I must to see it through.

Sample Menus

I am neither a medical doctor or nutritionist. I am just sharing a few sample meals for inspiration purposes. It's all based on my personal nutrition needs, taste and preferences.

Day X
<u>1st Meal</u>
- Spicy tuna with fresh avocado
- Homemade pumpkin-oat bread with vegan butter
- Coffee with coconut milk and stevia extract

<u>Snack</u>
- Fresh kiwi

<u>2nd Meal</u>
- Baked sweet potato- sour cream- nutritional yeast
- Sautéed garlic-lemon Brussel sprouts
- Tea with lemon and erythritol

Day Y
<u>Breakfast</u>
- Ginger grapefruit shot
- Oatmeal W/ coconut milk- strawberries- bananas...

<u>Lunch</u>
- Large salad: mixed greens- pine nuts- strawberries
- Dressing: balsamic vinegar- e.v. olive oil- salt- pepper
- Sugar free passionfruit sparkling lemonade

<u>Dinner</u>
- Split pea & squash soup with homemade croutons
- Frozen grapes

Day Z
1st Meal
- Coconut yogurt- maple syrup-blueberries & pineapple...
- Oat-flax biscuits with coconut manna
- Coffee sweetened with erythritol

2nd Meal
- Baked codfish with golden potatoes
- Sliced beets and boiled eggs was
- Sparkling water with lemon

Avocado Tuna W/ Pumpkin Bread...

Baked Codfish-Potato W/ Beets...

Healthier Choices

"The reason I exercise is for the quality of life I enjoy." Kenneth H. Cooper

The truly amazing thing about positive changes, is that it often only takes one positive act to create the domino effect. That journey to a healthier ME, did not end with me just cultivating healthier eating habits. No, its ripple effects could eventually be seen and felt throughout almost every area of my life. All of a sudden, I started approaching every decision the same way I proceeded with my nutrition plan. It's almost as if I became perpetually inclined to seek what was best for me, so I could develop healthier habits for everything.

Along with my new eating plan, I supplemented essential vitamins, accordingly. Soon after, I noticed hat I was naturally becoming more active. For instance, on the weekends, I would park my car further and further away, as I ran errands. A few months later, I started taking a 15-30 minute walk before and after work. Eventually, I increased that to a daily 45-60 minute speed-walking around my neighborhood. Then, when I found out that my company was paying for a personal trainer to work with employees in our gym, I signed-up, and swapped out my walks for customized sessions with the trainer, at least 3 days a week. Now, the truth is that working out consistently with the trainer after work, became the most challenging step for me. In fact, I briefly stopped going on several occasions, but kept being encouraged to continue by my then colleagues, Sheila and Marie. Though I must admit that the commitment and determination to their own sessions, inspired me more than anything else. So, I persevered; then after a while, it got easier, and surprisingly, even slightly enjoyable. Just slightly, because I'll never be one of those people who crave going to the gym... but I do love being active, and feeling invigorated!

Equally important, I became even more fiscally responsible. I had been keeping a monthly expense spreadsheet since I left my parents' home over a decade ago. Then a few years ago, I discovered Dave Ramsey's budget app, called: "everydollar" and been using it ever since. I would highly recommend this app for its ease of use and interactive functions. It has helped me further streamlined all my expenses to the bare essentials. I must remarked here, that another benefit of cooking most of my meals, is that it also increases my overall savings. Which enabled me to easily make personal loans towards my business startup costs in the past. The overall benefits of good financial decisions, are truly endless.

——

About 2 years into that journey, I collaborated with my physicians to run a complete blood work, and was ecstatic to hear about the results. All my concerned conditions had been pretty much reversed, and everything else got even better. The chronic inflammation was pretty much gone; all my vitamins went up to optimal level. I no longer suffered heartburn and nausea. For the first time in years, I was freed of my acne. As we continued to review and compare my new results to those from the prior 10-12 years, I made a promise to myself right then, that I would never return to my previous lifestyle.

Positive Lifestyle

"If you don't like the road you're walking, start paving another one." Dolly Parton

I had gotten in the habit of reflecting back on the freeing act that changed it all, and was always glad that I had decided to pave a healthier path for my life. The further I traveled onto that transformative path... the more engaging and focus that my lifestyle became. It's been marvelous to both observed and experienced that level of positive health. Consequently, I am very devoted to maintain and safeguard that state of being.

——

Now, don't get me wrong, the normal ups and downs of daily life still happened, as will always be the case for every living thing. I had just simply gotten into the flow of living a solution-focused lifestyle. Whenever something happened, I acknowledged it, then quickly shifted my focus on how best to resolve whatever it was. Funny enough, that was always kind of my general philosophy in life, but that mentality has been amplified by this journey. You know what I mean? Which is probably why I believe that we are all born with everything that we'll ever need within us; certain things just take longer to be activated, based on our personal choices.

Weight Loss

"We are what we repeatedly do, excellence therefore is not an act but a habit" Aristotle

By now, you are probably wondering if I might have just accidentally forgot to mention weight loss... well, not at all. On the contrary, I deliberately kept it out of all those previously listed positive changes, because I don't think that weight loss should ever be the only or primary goal for anyone, but rather a byproduct of long-term lifestyle changes. Yes, over these past 5-6 years, I have indeed shed any extra weight, and still continue to get more fit. Though for me, that was more like the delicious icing on the cake; sugar free icing of course.

In any case, I truly believe that focusing on implementing healthy eating and positive lifestyle habits, makes it easier for us to stick to a personalized nutrition guide, instead of just mindlessly following the current diet trends or obsessions. Chasing the instant gratification of those trending diets, can even be very harmful to our health. However, I know that it is easier said than done. Mostly in part to how good it can feel to see that dwindling number on the scale, or better yet to fit into that special sexy little black dress... but that often only leads to superficial and short-term satisfaction. As I mentioned earlier, I really don't ever want to get back to that unhealthy feeling, so I personally will always favor a slow but long-term progress, over any quick and short-term results. Like that saying goes, none of us gained all the weight in one day, so we'll never lose it in one day. Therefore, let's try to be kind and patient with ourselves on this beautifully flawed journey, we call life.

Lessons Learned

In the words of the always inspiring Ms. Oprah Winfrey, here's some of what I have learned for sure:

- Once you're truly ready for change; your resilience and determination will surprise even you.
- Identify your "why" before starting anything; it will help you stay the course when things seem unbearable.
- Every single human being is indeed capable of great change; stop blocking your own potential.
- Love bread & pizza? Learn how to make them with good ingredients, and share with loved ones. Nothing like it!

Homemade with clean ingredients

- Hurdles are inevitable, but you'll be the better for them.
- Always go for substance over superficiality. It's cool to fit the dress for a party but even better to be healthy.
- Don't copy, but rather be inspired by other people's weight loss journey and success, to create your own.
- Don't get caught up in weight loss amount, strive instead for a healthy size for your bone structure.
- Your authentic self will always be 10x better than the copy of anyone else; so become your own best version.
- Surround yourself with supportive family and friends; but be your own best devout cheerleader.
- A transformative journey is a marathon, not a sprint.
- Be flexible, everything happens for a reason.
- Like happiness, a healthy lifestyle is a personal and continuous choice.
- A healthy lifestyle should be the first and most important goal for every human being.

- Don't be so obsessive, that once in a while, you can't enjoy a piece of birthday cake. Life is all about balance!

——

I do think that life is meant to be lived and enjoyed in great health. Unfortunately, we are less likely to achieve that optimal health, if we just keep chasing instant gratification. So, why not dumped your kryptonite and say YES to a transformative adventure of your own. Who knows... perhaps along the way, you'll speed-walk right into a healthier YOU.

YOU CAN DO IT!

Judith is the founder & president of Business Development & Compliance Solutions, Inc. A business professional by day, content creator and podcast host by night. During these last 10 years, she's managed several great programs for the state of Florida in education, legal system, law enforcement compliance etc. She is the ultimate book nerd, and enjoys reading books from various genres in three languages. A New York girl at heart, she is a lover of pizza, train rides, classic movies, live performance. These days, when she is not writing in her tropical backyard, she can be found walking the Hollywood boardwalk and/or catching a nice sunset. She believes that happiness is a personal and continuous choice...

Printed in Great Britain
by Amazon